CARRIE INGALLS
The Forgotten Sister

written by
Clarissa Willis

illustrated by
Kashif Qasim

Copyright © 2025 Clarissa Willis
Cover art copyright © 2025 Clarissa Willis
All Rights Reserved

No part of this book may be reproduced or transmitted in any form or by any means, electronic or mechanical, including photocopying, recording, or by any information storage and retrieval system, without permission in writing from the author.

Library of Congress Number: 2025921930

Cover Art, – Kashif Qasim
Book Design – Sharon Kizziah-Holmes

SOLANDER
—PRESS—
Springdale, Arkansas

ISBN: 978-1-966675-56-3 (Paperback)
ISBN: 978-1-966675-55-6 (Hardback)
ISBN: 978-1-966675-57-0 (eBook)

Dedication

To my grandmother, Clara Urrey Brown, and my mother, Clarice Hightower, the most resilient women I have ever known.

Acknowledgments

Thank you so much to my critique partners, Margarite Stever, Lois Curran, Susan Keene, and Jen Kenning.

Thank you, Sharon Kizziah-Holmes, for being my book designer and friend.

CONTENTS

Dedication
Acknowledgments
Chapter 1
    Uncle Sam is Rich Enough 1
Chapter 2
    Across the Frozen Lake 5
Chapter 3
    A Baby Brother 9
Chapter 4
    The Fire and the Next School 13
Chapter 5
    The Railroad and Another New Town 17
Chapter 6
    A Single Bag of Wheat 21
Chapter 7
    Carrie Grows Up 25
Chapter 8
    The Landowner 29
Chapter 9
    The Proof King of South Dakota 33
Chapter 10
    A New Job and a New Life 37
Glossary 41
Resources 43
About the Author 45
About the Illustrator 47

CHAPTER I

Uncle Sam is Rich Enough

The headline "Uncle Sam Is Rich Enough to Give Us All a Farm" drew the attention of people across the country. Families could head west and claim 160 acres of free land. So, in 1868, the Ingalls family sold their farm and moved to Kansas.

The Ingalls family had four members: Charles, Caroline, his wife, and their two daughters, Mary and Laura. They traveled in a covered wagon from their home in the "Big Woods" of Wisconsin. The area was called the "Big Woods" because the forests stretched to the Mississippi River in the west and Lake Superior in the north.

They traveled across Minnesota and on through Iowa and Missouri before finally arriving in Kansas. Charles selected a plot of land in Rutland Township, Montgomery County, Kansas. Unfortunately, he was unaware that the land he picked was unavailable to homesteaders. He had chosen land on the Osage Indian Reservation.

Charles was so eager to start his farm that he never filed a legal claim on his land. He built a small cabin. The family worked together to make their farm successful. There was little time for playing because creating a homestead on the prairie was a full-time job. The grasslands were difficult to plow, and Charles labored to get the land ready to plant crops.

Two years later, on a hot day on the Kansas prairie, Charles Ingalls decided his two daughters, Laura and Mary, needed a day off. He took them on a long walk across the land to see an abandoned Osage Indian camp. The Indians were away on a hunting trip, and he wanted the girls to see the camp before they returned.

They left his wife, Caroline, at home, sitting in the shade and visiting with a neighbor, Mrs. Scott. Caroline was expecting a baby but was not due for a few weeks.

Life on the prairie was hard, and everyone, including the children, often worked from sunup to sundown doing chores. So, a day off was rare, and a visit from a neighbor was also a special treat.

When the family arrived home at sunset, a surprise

awaited them. Ma cradled a tiny, sleeping baby girl in her arms. Laura and Mary were so excited to have a baby sister.

Caroline Celestia Ingalls was born on August 3, 1870, thirteen miles from Independence, Kansas. She was the youngest child of Charles and Caroline Ingalls. From the start, she was described as a "sickly baby". Many babies did not survive infancy because of the harsh living conditions on the prairie. Even though she was frail and small, Carrie survived. She had two big sisters who gladly helped take care of her.

Like her older sisters, Carrie often enjoyed falling asleep while Ma sang to her.

> Hush, my babe, lie still and slumber,
> Holy angels guard thy bed,
> Heavenly blessings without number
> Gently resting on thy head.

When she was two weeks old, the census taker came to make a record of the family. Every ten years, all families in the United States are counted. In an era before widespread standardized records, census takers wrote names as they heard them, often leading to misspellings, even for literate families like the Ingalls.

According to the 1870 census-taker for Kansas, Ingles was recorded as the family name, although the spelling was incorrect. The household was listed as

C.P. (Charles), C (Caroline), and three children, M (Mary), age 5, L (Laura), age 3, and a two-week-old infant.

Eventually, the Osage people were forced to move to a new reservation, and the land was opened to settlers. Still, because of his haste in starting a homestead, Charles Ingalls' claim remained unofficial. Without proof of ownership, another family could have claimed their property.

Uncle Sam may have been wealthy enough to give pioneers free land, but holding on to it was another story. Little did they know that their two-week-old baby, Carrie, would later in life become an advocate for land ownership for homesteaders.

The Ingalls family, including Baby Carrie, watched as the long line of Native Americans on foot and horses passed their cabin on the way to their new home. With the Osage gone, the family had planned to stay in Kansas. One day, a letter arrived that changed everything.

CHAPTER 2

Across the Frozen Lake

Before leaving Wisconsin, Charles Ingalls sold his farm to Gustaf Gustafson. The letter that had arrived was from him. He could no longer afford the farm. The family had no choice but to leave Kansas and return to Wisconsin. If they didn't, the land they owned in Wisconsin would be sold to the highest bidder. With that in mind, they joined a wagon train headed back to Wisconsin. Carrie was not even a year old when she took the risky journey with her family as they traveled back to the "Big Woods" of Wisconsin.

Many weeks later, when they arrived at their farm, they discovered that the Gustafson family was still living there. Luckily, Caroline's sister and her family, Uncle Henry and Aunt Polly Quiner, lived nearby and invited the family to stay with them until the Gustafson family packed up and moved west. Carrie and her sisters had four cousins to play with: Louisa, Charley, Albert, and Lottie.

Other family members, including Grandma and Grandpa Ingalls, welcomed the family back to Wisconsin. Uncle Peter Ingalls and Aunt Eliza visited and brought four more cousins: Peter, Alice, Ella, and Edith.

Eventually, Charles and the rest of the family moved back to their cabin. Barry Corner School was near their home. Mary was now six and old enough to go to school. The following fall, Laura joined her, leaving Carrie alone all day with Ma.

Carrie never attended Barry Corner School because in February 1874, Charles sold the farm again. A Swedish farmer named Anderson paid $1,000. Pa and Uncle Peter always talked about going west. So before long, three-year-old Carrie joined her family and Uncle Peter's family on another long trip. This time, they traveled to Minnesota.

They left in February to cross Lake Pepin while it was still frozen and could support the weight of a covered wagon. They made the risky journey across the frozen lake in a heavy wagon, knowing the ice might break and they could all drown in the icy water. The weather was harsh, and the trail was rough. Riding in the back of the wagon was uncomfortable for the children. The first town they reached was Lake City, Minnesota. The severe weather stopped their journey westward.

The two families realized they needed to find shelter for the winter or risk freezing to death on the trail. Luckily, they found an abandoned cabin near Lake City and moved in together. With supplies from their covered wagons and meat from hunting local game, both families stayed dry and warm. They all had plenty to eat until spring.

Soon, the days started getting a little warmer, and the snow on the ground melted. It was finally spring. Uncle Peter's family stayed in eastern Minnesota, while the Ingalls family continued westward alone.

One evening, as they were getting ready to stop for the night, the unfamiliar sound of a loud whistle pierced the air. Ma told the girls that it was a train whistle. From their wagon, the children saw a train for the first time. They watched as it sped across the tracks.

Laura later wrote, "We were all silent, watching till the train was out of sight. Pa said we were living in a great age. He said a train could travel farther in one day than a covered wagon in a week. Pa spoke of railroads someday conquering the Great American Desert."

Each day, the family moved farther west, and each night, they camped. After supper, Pa played his fiddle and sang while the family sat beside the campfire.

Many days were long and tedious, while others were filled with pouring rain and muddy trails.

The three sisters had to get out and walk beside the wagon to prevent it from getting stuck in the deep mud. Finally, the family arrived in Walnut Grove, Minnesota.

Walnut Grove was a new town with only a few stores and houses. Pa built a dugout house and claimed 172 acres of prairie land. A dugout house is built by digging into the ground, usually on a hill. It has a flat roof and no windows. The dugout only had one room. A small stove was used both for cooking and staying warm.

Since their house was close to Walnut Grove, the Ingalls family helped establish the Union Congregational Church. They became friends with the pastor, Reverend Edward Alden, and his family.

On December 20, 1874, the church held a Christmas celebration, and the children saw their first Christmas tree. As part of the celebration, candles were lit and placed on the branches, and the children made paper ornaments to hang on the tree.

CHAPTER 3

A Baby Brother

By Carrie's fifth birthday, Pa had built a new cabin to replace their one-room dugout. Their new home had windows, and several rooms. The family seemed to thrive. However, this prosperity didn't last long, as a swarm of grasshoppers invaded the farm. What remained was the barren ground. All the crops were gone. The farmers of Walnut Grove, including the Ingalls family, lost everything. They had no income or food for the upcoming winter.

Charles left his family behind. He walked over 200 miles to find work. He wrote letters to tell them he had found work helping harvest crops in eastern Minnesota.

They looked forward to his letters even though they described the hard work and the long hours he spent in the fields.

When he returned, the family decided to move into town for the winter, so Mary and Laura could attend school. With the money he earned, Charles rented a small house behind the church in Walnut Grove.

In the fall of 1875, Mary and Laura returned to school. Carrie watched her sisters and the other children walk to school each day. She was still too young to go, so she stayed behind alone.

Imagine how excited Carrie was when Ma gave birth to a little boy four months after her fifth birthday. Carrie, Laura, and Mary now have a baby brother. They named him Charles Frederick Ingalls (Freddie). From the beginning, Freddie was sick.

The family missed their cabin on Plum Creek outside of town, so they moved back home as soon as the snow melted. Charles planted a new crop, and the family hoped the 1876 growing season would be prosperous and that the swarms of destructive grasshoppers would be gone for good.

Unfortunately, the grasshoppers had laid eggs in the soil, and the summer of 1876 was a repeat of 1875 as swarms of insects devoured every living plant and tree in the area. The family faced the hardship of no crops to sell for two years, a sick baby, and no way to survive another winter.

As they looked out on the barren fields and ruined

landscape, they knew Walnut Grove was no longer where Charles could support his family. He would have to give up his dream of farming and find a new job.

He was well known for his carpentry skills, and soon, he got a job helping remodel a hotel in Burr Oak, Iowa. He could work at the hotel, and Caroline could help run the hotel kitchen. This new job meant that the family would have a place to live at the hotel. Once again, they packed the wagon and moved.

The job didn't start until fall, and the family needed a place to stay. They headed to Uncle Peter's farm in eastern Minnesota for the summer. The girls missed their cousins and enjoyed playing with children again.

Everyone hoped that the warm weather would help baby Freddie get stronger. But he got sicker, and there was nothing anyone could do to help him.

During the hot summer days, baby Freddie grew weaker and weaker. He died on August 27, 1876. The children mourned with their parents over the loss of their little brother. Carrie was only six, but she seemed to struggle a lot with his death.

They buried Freddie near Uncle Peter Ingall's house. It was a tough time for everyone. The family of six once again became a family of five. It was especially difficult for Charles because he had always wanted a son.

In early fall, the family packed their wagon and headed to Burr Oak, Iowa. The trip was tough because everyone felt the impact of leaving Freddie behind.

Burr Oak was unlike any place they had lived before. At one time, it had been a hub for wagons heading west. There were two hotels and several stores in town. It appeared to the children to be bustling with activity.

While the Ingalls settled into the hotel, Carrie joined her sisters at Burr Oak School. She loved going to school, and her first teacher was Miss Sarah Donlan. Carrie did well in school, and with the help of her sisters, she soon learned to read.

Every night, she practiced her reading while her sisters did their homework. Mary often read to both Laura and Carrie. Ma and Pa encouraged the girls to do well in school, and from a young age, Laura wanted to become a teacher like Miss Donlan.

They spent their first Christmas in Burr Oak sledding down the hill near the hotel where they lived. Carrie and her sisters still missed Freddie.

CHAPTER 4

The Fire and the Next School

Helping with the hotel was a family job. Ma worked in the kitchen and helped keep the hotel clean while Pa did repairs. Mary, Laura, and Carrie all helped their parents with chores. They often helped make beds and clean hotel rooms. They knew many people who stayed at the hotel, including Mr. William Reid, the principal at their school. In those days, it was common for single people to live in a hotel.

When a saloon was built next to the hotel, Charles and Caroline became anxious about their three daughters growing up near a disgraceful place. Saloons were known for their loud music and fistfights between drunk customers.

Soon, the family found some rooms above a store and moved farther down the street from the saloon. As they slept one night, they were awakened by the smell of smoke. The saloon down the street was engulfed in flames. Then, the fire spread to the surrounding buildings. While their building did not burn, the Ingalls family decided living in town was not for them, so they moved again.

Pa found a cozy brick house on the edge of Burr Oak, and by early spring, the family moved in. On May 23, 1877, Caroline gave birth to a healthy baby girl with blonde hair like Mary's and blue eyes like Pa's. They named her Grace Pearl Ingalls. Six-year-old Carrie had a new sister.

She was excited that she was no longer the family's "baby" and that she had the chance to be Grace's "big sister". She would help her learn new things, just as Mary and Laura had helped Carrie when she was younger.

Burr Oak looked crowded and dirty to Pa Ingalls, and he still dreamed of taking his family west. One early fall morning in 1877, the family loaded the wagon and headed west again to Walnut Grove. The girls rode in the back of the wagon, and baby Grace was carried in Caroline's arms.

With winter fast approaching, they needed a place to live. They moved in with family friends, the Ensigns, who had three children: Willard, Anna, and Howard. The Ensign children formed lifelong friendships with Mary,

Laura, and Carrie. It was common for frontier families to "double-up" and live together.

All six children attended school together and shared the same books. In the spring, Pa bought some land and started building a cabin for his family. By summer, they had moved in. In the evenings, Pa would play his fiddle while the girls danced around, and Ma sang familiar tunes.

With the grasshopper days behind them, Walnut Grove prospered. Pa found work as a carpenter, and when he noticed the town didn't have a butcher shop, he opened one. The Ingalls family became active members of the Walnut Grove community; they attended church and took part in many local events.

In 1879, the residents of Walnut Grove discussed the railroad and its expansion into the Dakota Territory. However, the Ingalls family had little time to discuss the railroad, as the winter before Carrie's ninth birthday, Mary became sick with "Brain Fever".

Brain fever was the term the doctor used to describe her condition. What started as a headache and fever quickly made the doctor believe that Mary might not survive.

Carrie and Laura faced the possibility of losing another sibling. Being the oldest child, Mary had helped them learn to read and had always been a vital part of their lives. There were no medications to reduce the fever, and many people died from diseases that today could be easily cured.

Although Mary eventually recovered, she was blind and would never regain her sight. This affected the family and was a hardship they would deal with for years.

There were very few schools for blind children, and Mary, the sister who cared for Laura and Carrie, now became dependent on them for simple things. She needed help eating, dressing, and walking from place to place. Mary had always been a big help with chores, and now that too fell to Laura and Carrie.

CHAPTER 5

The Railroad and Another New Town

Work was scarce, and while Charles wanted to move westward and farm, he had no money. The U.S. government was offering land to homesteaders, but he had already learned the hard way that land alone wasn't enough to survive. He needed money to buy tools, livestock, and build a house for his family.

The answer to their problems came from Docia Forbes, his sister. She visited and told Charles that her husband, Hi Forbes, was a railroad contractor looking for someone to manage a company store. Each railroad camp had a store where the workers could use the money they earned working on the railroad to buy food and supplies.

Charles gladly accepted the job. Caroline was worried about how a blind child like Mary would manage another move. Charles assured her he would send money when it was time to move again, and Caroline and the four girls could ride the train to meet him at the end of the line in Tracy.

In September, Pa met the family as they stepped off the train. From there, they got into a covered wagon and traveled 40 miles west to the railroad camp where Charles worked. They moved to Silver Lake Camp when the work was finished at Big Sioux Camp. These camps were part of the Dakota Central Railroad.

Silver Lake Camp closed for the winter on December 1, 1879, but the foreman told the Ingalls family that if they stayed there over the winter and made sure none of the railroad's property was stolen, they could live in the surveyor's house.

Much to their surprise, when they moved into the two-story house, they found it stocked with food, nice furniture, and enough coal to last the winter. The family spent the winter of 1879-1880 in relative comfort.

The Ingalls turned their borrowed house into a business as settlers arrived in the Dakota Territory. Many homesteaders slept on the downstairs floor of their house, and the Ingalls' home became an informal stop for families heading west. To earn extra money for the family, Caroline Ingalls served meals for a quarter in the large dining area.

The Ingalls family was excited when Reverend Edward Alder and his wife from Walnut Grove stayed at their makeshift boarding house during the winter of 1880. They had come west to establish a church in De Smet, South Dakota. The first service was held on February 29, 1880. The Ingalls family was the congregation. They conducted the first service in the parlor of the surveyor's house where the Ingalls lived.

By February 1880, Charles realized it was time to stake his own claim for the land offered by the government. He rode into Brookings, where he put in a claim for 160 acres near De Smet, in the Dakota Territory.

Settlers could pay $1.60 per acre or become homesteaders by living on the land for five years. After that time, the family would own the land free and clear. Charles was a homesteader because he did not have enough money to buy the land outright.

His property was right outside the settlement that would become De Smet. When he selected his land, there wasn't much in the tiny settlement of De Smet.

The small town was named after a Catholic priest who had been a missionary to the Sioux Indians. But soon, settlers poured in from the east, helped by the new railroad line, and De Smet began to grow.

On March 1, 1880, Laura and Carrie walked into De Smet to look around. Carrie's trip was very disappointing. She expected to see a bustling town.

Carrie complained that all she saw was a bunch of sticks in the ground. Ma explained the sticks were there to show where buildings would be built.

Ma and Pa Ingalls, on the other hand, were very excited to settle down and become part of the Dakota territory. They had lived in many places, and as the girls grew older, they knew it was time to settle down and stay in one place. They wanted Laura and Carrie to have the opportunity to make friends and go to school.

They still worried about Mary, who, as a blind teenager, had little prospect of ever becoming independent. They hoped that De Smet would be their final stop on the long journey west.

Unfortunately, the Ingalls family was very unprepared for what they would face in the new town.

CHAPTER 6

A Single Bag of Wheat

When the railroad returned in mid-March 1880, Carrie's family needed a place to live. Charles used old lumber from the railroad camp to build a store in De Smet. The family lived above it for a few months.

When the railroad workers finished laying the tracks, the train arrived in De Smet. It was a growing community. Two stores, a hotel, a church, and a school were under construction. While Charles' store was thriving, he was eager to leave the busy city and return to farming.

Charles abandoned his store and built a one-room shanty on his land, and the family moved there in late summer. The shanty was tiny. Caroline said, "It looks like half a woodshed that had been split along the ridgepole."

The family quickly got busy at their new homestead. They dug a well and built a shelter for the livestock. Caroline and her girls planted a garden. Even though Carrie had just turned ten, she learned to help with the never-ending chores.

The hot summer days cooled down as fall approached. Suddenly, winter arrived, and the one-room shanty became too cold for the family. They had planned to stay there until later in the winter, but Mother Nature had other plans.

On October 15, 1880, a fierce blizzard struck the Dakota Territory. It soon became clear that the Ingalls family could not survive the coming winter in a one-room shanty.

First, Charles took his haystacks to town in the wagon. Then he returned to the shanty, and he and Caroline packed the wagon with their few pieces of furniture, bedding, and clothes. They returned to town and moved back into the rooms above the small store Charles had built. The good news was that Laura and Carrie could go to school.

A lot had changed over the summer while they lived in the shanty. The school had been completed and opened on November 1, 1880. Laura and Carrie were two of the first fifteen students to attend De Smet School. When another blizzard hit during a school day,

Laura and Carrie struggled to find their way back to where they lived.

Settlers depended on the train for their supplies. Not only did they get food delivered daily by train, but they also received mail and, most importantly, coal for fuel. Charles and the other men from town often shoveled snow from the tracks so the train could reach the station.

As the blizzards continued into January 1881, the railroad made a decision that significantly affected Carrie and her family. They would not deliver more supplies until spring and would cease operations for the winter.

The school was shut down because there wasn't enough coal to keep the children warm, and soon food became scarce in the town. Food prices rose sharply, with flour costing $50 a pound, and the last few pounds of sugar selling for $1 a pound. Without coal, the Ingalls burned hay twisted into bundles. As their kerosene ran low, they burned the oil lamps less and less at night. But a good deed by Charles may have saved the family.

Two brothers who owned a store, Ross and Almanzo Wilder, grew wheat on a farm outside of town. Charles helped them bring it into town and store it in the back of their shop. While the brothers sold hay to the other townspeople, they kept their wheat supply a secret because they knew that wheat seed might not arrive in time for spring planting with the railroad shut down. To thank Charles for his help, the brothers sold him a bag of their valuable wheat.

That wheat may have saved the Ingalls family from starvation. For months, they lived on brown bread made from flour ground with the seed wheat in the coffee mill. This period of malnutrition took a toll on Carrie's already fragile health, and she never fully recovered.

However, the Ingalls family survived while many others did not. With no food stored for the winter, no coal being brought in by the railroad, and no connection to the outside world, more than one family died of starvation and exposure to the harsh elements. By the time the snow melted and the railroad returned to De Smet, the town's population had decreased significantly.

CHAPTER 7

Carrie Grows Up

One day, Reverend Alden visited the family. He told them he had a relative working at the school for the blind in Vinton, Iowa. This was a chance for Mary to attend a special school and learn to live more independently. In the fall of 1881, Mary enrolled in the College for the Blind in Iowa. Laura became a teacher to help the family with expenses.

Carrie graduated from high school in 1888. Since teaching was one of the few respectable jobs for a woman, Carrie studied hard and passed the teacher's exam. Like her sister, Laura, she became a teacher in De Smet. But unlike Laura, who loved teaching, Carrie found it boring.

In 1889, while still a teenager, Carrie began training for a new profession that would define the rest of her working life: the newspaper business. She got a job as an apprentice with Carter P. Sherwood of the *De Smet Leader*.

Carrie felt full of energy and purpose in the bustling newspaper office, with its smell of ink and the clatter of the press. This very laborious job required a lot of time and patience. Each letter had to be positioned by hand. Later, as newspaper production expanded, molds were created from the typeset pages and used to make a printing plate.

In 1884, a new machine called the Linotype was invented. It allowed the operator or typesetter to compose an entire line of text by typing on a machine. In a small rural newspaper office like the one where Carrie worked, expensive new machines like the Linotype were rare. Most typesetters, including Carrie, likely set each letter by hand.

Carrie learned to produce a newspaper by placing each letter onto a printing plate one at a time. For the newspaper to be printed correctly, every letter had to be placed in the exact order and lined up perfectly.

During her apprenticeship at the *De Smet Leader* newspaper, she earned one dollar a week. In addition to setting type, she learned how to create advertising and occasionally wrote articles for the paper.

In 1881, the *De Smet Leader* and the *Kingbury County News* merged. A surviving photo shows the newspaper staff standing outside the office. Three unidentified men and one woman (Carrie Ingalls) were photographed.

Newspapers did much more than print the news. They also offered printing services for stationery, forms, and books. Since South Dakota had only recently become a state, forms were necessary. Carrie's articles ranged from personal stories to historical topics. Advertising was a major source of income for a newspaper, and she enjoyed planning and designing advertisements.

Another vital role of the local newspaper was posting notices such as births, deaths, and land claims. Homesteaders like Almanzo Wilder (Laura's husband) had to prove they settled and lived on their land. Placing a notice in the newspaper became the most effective way to make land claims official.

Today, we are used to receiving news instantly. However, in the 1880s, news from around the country was often delayed by days or weeks. While major national events were typically printed in newspapers, most rural papers relied on local news for their content. The length of time Carrie worked for the *Kingsbury Independent Newspaper* is not precisely known, but it was roughly five years. During this time, she lived at home.

In 1902, Charles Ingalls died, and the family faced the grief of losing their pa. Carrie stayed at home with her mother and sister, Mary, until 1905.

Single and with no prospects for a husband, Carrie traveled. Because of her ongoing health issues, she went to Boulder, Colorado, hoping the warmer weather would help her asthma.

Later, she visited relatives in Minnesota. She worked in the newspaper business as a freelance author. It was common for newspapers to pay for stories or features written by people who did not work for the paper.

CHAPTER 8

The Landowner

Although the exact dates of her other jobs are unknown, she worked as a substitute teacher, a retail clerk, and at the Post Office. Her travels also took her farther west to places like Wyoming. No matter what she did during those years, she always seemed to return to South Dakota.

When she returned to South Dakota, it was time for another significant milestone in her life. One that was typically reserved for men. Carrie became a female homesteader and property owner.

Two important historical events impacted the next chapter in Carrie's life. First, the government set up a land lottery where people could enter a drawing to gain land for homesteading. Those who didn't want to take their chances with a lottery could buy a tract of land outright as long as they met a residency requirement. The second historical event was that this land was no longer available only to men; women could purchase land, too.

As new families moved westward, they soon learned that to own land, they had to "prove it up". The term "prove up" the land meant they had to make improvements on the land, build a livable structure (house, shack, cabin), and either farm it or keep livestock on it. To achieve this, the landowner had to either live on the land for five years or pay a fee and own the land after fourteen months of occupancy.

Carrie decided she wanted to be a landowner. Her tract of land was near Topbar, South Dakota. She lived in a one-room tar-paper shack approximately 10 feet long and 12 feet wide.

Tar-paper was a cheap alternative to wood. The shacks usually had a wooden frame with waterproof paper stretched across it. They were supposed to be used for temporary housing but were often used in the rural south and western parts of the United States as primary living spaces.

Carrie's tar-paper shack had a coal stove inside for warmth and cooking. She lived there for six months during the spring and summer but returned to De Smet for the winter. She knew firsthand how brutal the South Dakota winters could be.

Her mother and sister, Mary, lived in De Smet, and she moved in with them for the winter months. However, as soon as the snow melted, she traveled 20 miles back to her land to complete her residency requirement.

She returned to her tar-paper shack in the spring and lived there for eight more months, completing her required fourteen-month residency. She was now eligible to be a verified landowner, a remarkable accomplishment for a single woman.

The next step was to pay fifty cents an acre, totaling $80 for the 160-acre tract. The paperwork took quite a while to reach Washington, D.C. and be recorded. By 1909, she was an official landowner.

This was very unusual when most land was owned by men who planned to farm or raise livestock. Carrie saw this land as her investment in the future.

Even though she was a property owner, Carrie now faced the need to support herself, so she returned to what she enjoyed most: working for a newspaper. She had spent years learning how to set type, edit, design advertisements, and manage the financial records for a local paper.

While some women did work in the newspaper business, very few knew how to do all those tasks. That hard work paid off when she had a chance meeting with a business owner known for his talent for making money in the newspaper industry.

The exact date is uncertain, but sometime while working for a few months at a newspaper in Arlington, South Dakota, Carrie Ingalls met businessman E. L. Senn. That meeting would shape the rest of her life.

CHAPTER 9

The Proof King of South Dakota

Carrie got a job at the *Arlington Sun* in Arlington, South Dakota, about 20 miles east of De Smet.

The editor H.M. Keene posted an announcement in the paper: "Miss Carrie Ingalls of De Smet has taken a place in *The Sun* office. Miss Ingalls has recently proved up a piece of land not far from Cottonwood and refuses to sell it, believing that she will double her money on the investment within a year or two."

Carrie was the shop foreman and handled many aspects of the newspaper, including designing the advertising. She held this job for only a few months before returning to De Smet.

It is unknown why she only stayed a short time at the job; perhaps it was too far away from her homestead, or maybe she needed a more challenging job. But one good thing about her work there was meeting Mr. E.L. Senn.

E.L. Senn was often called the "final proof" king. He made his fortune by buying newspapers and charging homesteaders to publish their final proof documents in his papers.

These "final proofs" served as written evidence that a homesteader had fulfilled the requirements for land ownership. Each settler had to publish an announcement in their local paper for five weeks, stating their intention to make proof (secure the legal title) for their land.

These proof notices needed to include witnesses who could testify that the homesteader had met the government's requirements.

Think of it as a public announcement. Before a homesteader could receive the official deed to their land, they had to prove they had lived there. Publishing a notice was their way of shouting, "This land is mine!"

Newspapers competed to be able to publish these documents because they were a significant source of income for the papers. By 1907, Carrie was thirty-seven and working for Mr. Senn in Pedro, South Dakota, just a few miles from her land claim. She performed various tasks, including typesetting the paper and designing advertisements, another revenue stream for rural newspapers.

Senn, a ruthless businessman, hired women to work on his newspapers because he felt they were hard workers. His newspapers primarily published legal notices, but later expanded to cover local news. Carrie was a good fit for his newspapers as a woman and a landowner. Being single made it easy for her to move from place to place whenever Senn bought another newspaper.

By 1909, Carrie had established herself as a premier editor, typesetter, and contributor to several South Dakota newspapers. She was known as a hard worker with an eye for detail.

During this time, she became the editor of the *Pedro Bugle*, a very prestigious job, especially for a woman. However, the town soon faced hardships. The once-thriving town had dwindled to only 16 residents and three businesses. One reason was that once land in a specific area was owned free and clear, the need to publish five-weekly notices disappeared. The paper soon became unnecessary since the land was all claimed, and the businesses didn't need to advertise.

Carrie's next editorial position was in 1910 at the *Roseland Review*. Her attention to detail made her skills desirable. Unlike Pedro, Roseland was thriving with homesteaders and new businesses. The newspaper's "final proof" business grew as those homesteaders became established.

Each "final proof" had to be published correctly; a simple error, like a misspelled word, would mean the homesteader had to wait until the evidence was republished, thus delaying their land ownership. Carrie recognized this and became known for her flawless production of "final proofs".

When claims for owning a mine, such as a gold mine or copper mine, were subjected to the same rules as homestead land, Mr. Senn saw another opportunity to make money. He bought newspapers in mining towns. Suddenly, he had an additional income source because miners now had to publish their claims just like homesteaders did. Who did he send to ensure the newspapers he purchased ran smoothly and efficiently? Carrie Ingalls.

CHAPTER 10

A New Job and a New Life

Carrie arrived in Keystone, South Dakota, in 1911. Her job was to manage the *Keystone Recorder*. While homesteaders had to pay up to $5 for proof of land ownership, Senn raised the rates to $9 for mining claims. Five weeks of publishing such notices ($45) was a hefty sum in 1911. It is equivalent to over $1,500 today.

Keystone was a mining town in western South Dakota. As the town grew, it became one of the wealthiest areas in the state. Carrie's opportunity to manage the busy newspaper was both difficult and rewarding.

Newspapers printed death notices called obituaries. Before Carrie arrived in Keystone, an important obituary appeared in the paper. This was the obituary of Elizabeth Gordon Swanzey, the wife of David N. Swanzey.

The obituary on the front page of the paper read, "Elizabeth Swanzey was the young wife of a prominent citizen of Keystone. She died in childbirth at the age of 31."

David N. Swanzey owned over 30 mining claims and oil and uranium deposits. With all those legal ads to publish, he knew the paper's staff well, which is likely where he first saw Carrie.

By 1912, Carrie was in Hill City, South Dakota, running another newspaper. Imagine her surprise when David Swanzey traveled to Hill City to court her. Although she had long since given up hope of marrying, she accepted his proposal.

Two days before her forty-second birthday, Carie Ingalls married David Swanzey. She became the stepmother of Swanzey's two young children, Mary and Harold. She raised them and made sure they were well-educated and loved.

From the moment she married, she had her work cut out for her. Around 1910, both the Swanzey children, Mary and Harold, had contracted scarlet fever. As a result, Harold was deaf.

Carrie also became very active in the community. She was known as a kind and generous person. In 1920, she joined the Eastern Star, a women's organization, and represented them at their convention in Denver, Colorado.

David Swanzey was among the local leaders who helped the sculptor Gutzon Borglum select the mountain where he would carve his famous monument. One account says he may have been part of the group that gave Mount Rushmore its name. His son Harold worked on the project when he was a young adult.

Carrie Ingalls Swanzey exemplified the pioneer spirit. During her life, she was an independent woman, a landowner, a newspaper manager, and a traveler throughout the West.

Edith Kohl, who was also a female editor, once wrote, "Needles and thread and bread dough have done more toward preserving the nation than bullets, and the women who made homes on the prairie did more than any other group to establish the West." These early Western pioneer women had more rights and opportunities in the West than many imagined possible.

Carrie Ingalls went beyond traditional roles to become a leader in a predominantly male society. The "final proof" newspaper movement helped many homesteaders own land.

Yes, newspapers earned money from publishing the "final proofs", but more importantly, people without money gained unimagined opportunities. They could own land, and with that ownership, a new type of American appeared—fiercely independent and proud citizens who built communities that still thrive today.

In 1930, Carrie wrote a history of the town of De Smet, and there is one remaining poem she published:

> "Once on a blue, blue moon, you'll find
> A friend that is tried and true
> And perhaps once again you'll find
> A friend when the moon is turning blue
> But look no more but cherish them
> For a miracle to the last
> If you keep that friend as a true friend
> Till' the beautiful moon has passed."

Caroline "Carrie" Ingalls Swanzey may not have left behind writings or dramatic stories of hardship turned into triumph. But what she left is just as meaningful: an example of perseverance, quiet dedication, and inner strength. She lived through a time of significant social and technological change. She witnessed the transformation of the American West and made a lasting impact through her work, relationships, and resilience.

GLOSSARY

Apprentice: A person who agrees to work for low wages. They work for a fixed amount of time while learning a trade.

Census: Every ten years, the United States Government counts the number of people living in each geographical area of the country.

Census taker: A person who goes from house to house to find out how many people live in the household and their ages.

Coal stove: A stove used for heating or cooking that burns coal for fire. Coal stoves became popular in the late 1800s as an alternative to burning wood.

Dugout house: A dugout, also known as a pit house or earth lodge, is a shelter built by digging into the ground. Dugouts can be entirely covered with dirt or constructed into a hillside.

Final proof: The government used this term to determine whether a person had met the qualifications to own the land where they live. Each family had to print a notice five times in the newspaper stating they met the requirements to own the land. Then, the government issued them the deed to the property.

Homesteader: A family or group that lives on land and builds a shelter. Under the homestead laws, a settler had to live on the property for a given amount of time and build a house. In addition, the homesteader had to either farm the land or raise cattle on the land.

Obituary: A legal notice usually printed in the newspaper announcing the death of someone.

Pioneer: Someone who is one of the first to explore or live in a place. During the 19th century, American pioneers traveled to the West in covered wagons.

Prove up: A term used to describe how a homesteader would improve the land they were living on, either by farming, raising livestock, or building a home.

Tar-paper shack: A home made of water-resistant paper. Typically, these homes had no windows and offered little protection from hot or cold weather.

Typesetter: A person who worked for a newspaper or printer and put together the text for publication. In the 1800s and early 1900s, type was often placed into a mold one letter at a time, making it a very long and difficult task.

Uncle Sam: A name given to the United States (note it has the same first letter) to represent the American Government. It was like a nickname.

Resources

About Caroline "Carrie" Ingalls Swanzey | Little House on the Prairie.
https://littlehouseontheprairie.com/about-caroline-carrie-ingalls-swanzey/

Anderson, W. (1992). Laura Ingalls Wilder: *A Biography.* Harper Collins, New York, NY.

Anderson, W. (1971). *The Story of the Ingalls.* Anderson Publishing.

Herbert Hoover Presidential Library and Museum, West Branch, Iowa.

Kirkpatrick, J. (2022). Carrie Ingalls' South Dakota Life. South Dakota Public Broadcasting.

South Dakota Historical Society. Carrie Ingalls, https://history.sd.gov/

Williams, J.H. (2019). *Little Newspapers on the Prairie: The Frontier Press Career of Carrie Ingalls.* The Little Print Shop, Rapid City, SD.

Historical Biographies
by Clarissa Willis

Available at Amazon and
other online book retail outlets.

ABOUT THE AUTHOR

Award-winning author Clarissa Willis writes children's books. She has authored nine picture books and one chapter book. *Bloomers on Pike's Peak, the story of Julia Archibald Holmes*, received a Will Rogers Medallion Award and was a finalist for the Women Writing the West 2025 WILLA Literary Award in Children's Picture Books. Her book *Fast as the Wind: The Story of Johnny Fry Pony Express Rider* won a Will Rogers Medallion in 2023. *The Three Little Pigs and the Not So Big Bad Wolf* was released in early 2025. It tells a familiar story with a new twist. She believes childhood is a journey and strives to make it joyful through her books and public speaking.

Clarissa loves traveling and has a special connection to the American West. She finds inspiration in the red rocks of Sedona, Arizona, and the Rocky

Mountains of Colorado. In fact, her next book, *Not from Around Here*, is set in Sedona and chronicles an unusual friendship between a young cowboy and his friend from far away.

Connect with Clarissa at clarissa@clarissawillis.com and visit her website at www.clarissawillis.com.

About the Illustrator

Kashif Qasim is a professional artist. He has over 20 years of experience in children's book illustration, portraits, landscape art, and sculpture. Fluent in several languages, he works internationally with authors and is best known for his free-hand digital style.

www.ingramcontent.com/pod-product-compliance
Lightning Source LLC
LaVergne TN
LVHW050841080526
838202LV00009B/308